Advance Praise

"What happens to a woman who loses her name? This is one of the many questions Nancy Gerber asks about her maternal grandmother, the focus of her compassionate and moving memoir, *Burnt Toast.* It is an account of the profound and irreparable loss experienced by immigrants as they leave their home, parents, mother tongue—and even name—behind. With honesty, beauty, and humanity, Gerber details the strong bond forged between grandmother and granddaughter, who quietly connect through food, embroidery, their independent spirits, and an unspoken belief in each other. Ultimately, the book memorializes not only a portrait of Gerber's grandmother, but also many facets of the Jewish immigrant experience."

—Ellen Sherman, author of *Into the Attic*

"What does it mean not to carry your given name into your life in a new land? What does it do to the generations after to have no stories that were told of the lives left behind? How does this granddaughter make stories out of her deep and anguished love for this elder who didn't know or remember the time and place of her birth and childhood, truncated by war, pogroms, poverty and necessity? Nancy Gerber's *Burnt Toast: A Memoir of My Immigrant Grandmother*, sets before us a scene of memories she has made out of those lost to the generations before her who came from that geopolitical, mythical Pale of Settlement which has been, and remains, the site of historical traumas we must come to know."

— Frances Bartkowski, author of *An Afterlife*

"*Burnt Toast* is a moving journey through time as Nancy Gerber bears witness to her grandmother's unspoken trauma. Beginning with a young girl's survival of a deadly pogrom and her solo trip across the ocean, this memoir feels both personal and universal. Mining the rich soil beneath her grandmother's words, Gerber unearths the deep loss and abiding love that was long ago buried. She validates her grandmother, as well as any of us whose voices have been silenced. She clears a path toward "asylum from the ghosts of our past," and provides an emotional and thought-provoking read, not to be missed.

— Lisa A. Sturm, author of *Echoed in My Bones*

"In this heartfelt memoir, Nancy Gerber gives voice to the complexities of the immigrant experience: ruptures sustained, questions unanswered, and traumas borne across generations. Her vignettes glow with pathos, honesty, and the particular stoic melancholy of the American Jewish refugee."

— Rabbi Danny Moss, Temple Beth Tikvah

Burnt Toast

Burnt Toast

A Memoir of
My Immigrant Grandmother

Nancy Gerber

Apprentice House Press
Loyola University Maryland

"We Are All Refugees" was originally published in an eponymous chapbook by New Feral Press, 2017.

The section describing burnt toast (pages 11-12) appeared under the title "In Bessie's Kitchen" *in Adanna Literary Journal*, Issue 11, 2021.

First Edition

Library of Congress Control Number: 2022950111

Paperback ISBN 978-1-62720-478-1
Ebook ISBN 978-1-62720-479-8

Design by Kamryn Spezzano
Promotional development by Natalie Misyak
Editorial development by Caitlyn Jennings

Published by Apprentice House Press

Apprentice
House Press
Loyola University Maryland

Loyola University Maryland
4501 N. Charles Street, Baltimore, MD 21210
410.617.5265
www.ApprenticeHouse.com

info@ApprenticeHouse.com

For my family

If you do not know the names . . .
the knowledge of them is lost, too.
—Carl Linnaeus

Fly down, Death: Call me:
I have become a lost name.
—Muriel Rukeyser

This story begins with a woman who lost her name.
Her history, silenced.
Her language, abandoned. Thick, curling syllables
unwound from the mother's tongue.
Yiddish.
Mameloshn.
Translation: Mother Tongue.

This is the story of what I know and what I don't know about my maternal grandmother, born in the Ukraine sometime during the late 1890's. Persecuted, hunted like a rabbit, she was just eight years old when she survived a pogrom, crouched beneath her bed, cowering in fear as Cossack soldiers on horseback stampeded through the streets, murdering Jews in government-sponsored sport. At the age of 15 she fled her birthplace, leaving behind both everything and everyone she knew. Once she left, she never saw home again.

The New York Times described the pogroms of Easter 1903 in this way: "The anti-Jewish riots are worse than the censor will permit to publish. There was a well laid-out plan for the general massacre of Jews on the day following the Orthodox Easter. The mob was led by priests, and the general cry, 'Kill the Jews,' was taken up all over the city. The Jews were taken wholly unaware and were slaughtered like sheep. The dead number 120 and the injured about 500. The scenes of horror attending this massacre are beyond description. Babies were literally torn to pieces by the frenzied and bloodthirsty mob. The local police made no attempt to check the reign of terror. At sunset the streets were piled with corpses and wounded."

The terror of living through a pogrom must have stayed with her all her life. Babies wrenched from their mothers, torn into pieces.

She must have wondered how she survived.

She never spoke about her experience.

I don't know whose idea it was that she should leave home forever. Did she have a say in the decision? Was she pushed out by her parents through the force of their love, because to remain where she was would mean living with the constant threat of death?

My grandmother never said where she came from because she didn't really know. Uneducated, impoverished Jews were not wanted in her part of the world. When I asked her what country she was born in, she'd wave her hand in a gesture of dismissal: *Russia, Poland, who knows?* It didn't matter, it wasn't important to her, since her existence meant nothing to those who held the reins of power. To be a Jew in that place and time was to live on the murderous edge of extinction.

If you don't know where you come from, how do you know who you are?

For many years I believed my grandmother had been born in a shtetl, a small village inhabited by penniless Jews, to parents who lived in a thatched cottage surrounded by scrawny chickens scratching in the dirt. But according to the research of my mother's oldest brother, my grandmother was born in Ekaterinoslav. Where did she reside in the city named for Empress Catherine the Great, who established the Pale of Settlement?

The Pale, a western region of Imperial Russia from the years 1791 to 1917, was a place of shifting boundaries that included most of Poland. It was an area where Jews were granted permanent residency and beyond which Jews were mostly forbidden. It was a territory of almost 473,000 square miles. It was the world's largest ghetto.

A metropolis that flourished from the mining of coal and iron, Ekaterinoslav was the third city in the Russian Empire to boast trams. Jews were the city's third largest ethnic group at the end of the 19th century. The men were tradespeople: tailors, shoemakers, cabinet makers, jewelers. I imagine my grandmother may have been born in a humble dwelling with the aid of a midwife, just like her mother and her mother's mother and all the forgotten women who came before her. The details of her early life are lost to me. She was a girl on the wrong side of history. The lives of such girls are always invisible and unrecorded.

And what if my uncle was wrong? What if my grandmother was born in a tiny shtetl instead of in Ekaterinoslav? No one would remember this place because it no longer exists. Its existence was so precarious to begin with that nobody paid any attention when it finally disappeared, perhaps annihilated during the ravages of World War II. My grandmother was born somewhere in Russia—who really knows—and in 1910 (or thereabouts) she came to the United States of America, the Golden Land.

That much I do know. I know because I held my grandmother's gnarled fingers and studied her lined face and listened to her foreign voice, an English heavily inflected with Yiddish that was as much a part of her as her unknown, unknowable story.

A story she refused to share with me. To protect me, I assume. Or to stop me from asking too many questions, forcing her to relive a terrifying, traumatic past.

• • •

My grandmother came to America on a ship. There was no other way to travel halfway across the world during her time. I wonder what she wore on her voyage? Maybe a long woolen skirt, layers of warm sweaters, perhaps a kerchief to cover her head. My mother described to me a fifteen-year-old girl clutching a featherbed (or was it a coverlet? a blanket?), a small block of cured meat, and a few kopeks, a Russian form of currency.

And here's something else: she was completely alone.

My grandmother traveled in third class, in steerage, and she got sick. Everyone in steerage was suffering with the sickness that comes to those who cross the roiling seas.

But this was not first-class travel. Conditions were filthy. Buckets for the emptying of stomach and bowels. No running water. Illness everywhere. The stench was overwhelming. The strangers who huddled below deck eventually got used to it.

My grandmother menstruated for the first time on that huge heaving vessel and didn't know what was happening to her, my mother said. No one had told my grandmother what happens to young girls on the verge of womanhood. She thought she was dying. To be alone, so alone and so far from home, to bleed and bleed and believe you are dying.

And here's another thing: she never saw her mother, my great-grandmother, again.

• • •

My grandmother never spoke about any of this to me – her childhood, her mother, her passage to America. It was too painful to revisit the wounds of the past which bled and bled and never healed. What would be the point? She'd come to this place, the New World, to start over, to begin a new life. She pretended the old one never existed.

And I was a child. I did not realize my grandmother had a history before I was born.

Anything I know comes through my mother and the genealogical research of my uncle, which may or may not be reliable.

For many years I believed in the myth of America as a Golden Land, a place of endless freedom and opportunity. Who wouldn't want to come to America? To complain – about the loneliness, ostracism, anti-Semitism, grief, the loved ones left behind – such talk would have seemed profoundly ungrateful.

And un-American.

• • •

My grandmother was processed through immigration in a makeshift station on the pier of the harbor in Philadelphia, City of Brotherly Love, which at the time was the third largest port of entry for immigrants. Her heart was hammering so loudly she was certain everyone could hear it.

Then came interrogations and evaluations. A medical exam in a small, cold room, my grandmother stripped, trembling and ashamed in front of a group of strange men. Shy and modest, she had never once stood before a man in only her undergarments. Immigration officials eyed her up and down as if she were livestock.

Forms stamped. A new name. *This is America*, they said. *Here we speak English. From now on you will be called Bessie. A good American name.* The name her own mother bestowed on her, her truest name, erased forever. I don't know her true name and I never will. No one ever told me Bessie's true name and now there's no one left to ask.

History obliterated the name her mother gave her. There are no records or official documents with my grandmother's real name. On her marriage certificate her name is listed as Bessie Katz. But the records in Philadelphia list so many Bessie Katz's it's impossible to trace my grandmother among them.

It's likely that my grandmother's last name was not Katz.

What happens to a woman who loses her name?

Brown Bessie was a prized heifer at the 1893 Chicago World's Fair. Had the immigration men named my grandmother after a famous cow?

My grandmother went to live with her older sister, Ensa, in

Philadelphia.

What do I know of Ensa? She probably worked as a seamstress, perhaps in the same shop as Philip Siman, my grandfather, a tailor who worked for his oldest brother. The story goes that when Philip came courting Ensa he met my grandmother, the younger, prettier sister, and was smitten with her.

I like to imagine that moment when Bessie opened the front door to Philip. She was shorter than her older sister and slightly plumper, more *zaftig*. She wore a long, dark skirt and a white ruffled blouse, her dark curls just reaching the collar, her large eyes sparkling, illuminating her pale skin. There was a softness and yearning in her expression that appealed to Philip. Seeing her standing in that narrow passage he had the overwhelming urge to reach out and clasp her to his chest.

Philip and Bessie married on October 1, 1917, at City Hall in Philadelphia. In the Philadelphia Marriage Index their marriage was recorded by the Clerk of the Orphan's Court. And indeed, they were orphans. The mothers who gave birth to them, the fathers they called Papa – were never to be seen again in their entire lives. Philip and Bessie were married far from home, in a strange new land where their foreignness and their Jewishness and their poverty made them objects of suspicion and disdain.

One of my sons was able to trace Philip's given name from marriage and census records: Philip was born as Rafael Strikovsky. This information then helped my son locate the ship's manifest which records Philip's passage to the New World. But since my grandmother's given name is unknown, it is impossible to trace her journey.

Oddly, Ensa disappears from the family narrative. In the genealogical record of my uncle's research Ensa is not given a birth date nor a date of death. Did she marry and have children? Did she die of illness? Or from a broken heart when her younger sister stole her beau?

I am named for this cast-off sister. Ensa lives on in me through my given name, and yet I know nothing about her life, what she enjoyed, or even what kind of woman she was. And I also don't know whether she ever forgave my grandmother.

• • •

My grandmother never learned to read or write. She was illiterate.

Such an ugly word, illiterate. I prefer unlettered. To her dying day she signed her name with an X, for her signature. This mark was the only sign she could make on paper.

Grandmom, I write to honor that X. You are not crossed out. Can you hear me?

I write to remember you and affirm your struggle in all its beauty and suffering.

• • •

The 1920s were an era of virulent anti-Semitism in the United States. The racist and anti-Semitic Ku Klux Klan boasted four million members, just slightly less than the 4.2 million Jewish people. Justice Louis Brandeis, the first Jew to serve on the Supreme Court, endured anti-Semitic taunts from fellow Justice James McReynolds. Henry Ford, in his paper entitled *The Dearborn*, blamed Jews for all the economic ills facing America. Quotas restricted Jews from professions such as banking and insurance as well as entrance to professional training, including law and medical and dental schools. The rise of the white supremacist movement in 2016 revived the open expression of anti-Semitism in

Neo-Nazi activities, the display of swastikas, the bombing of the Pittsburgh synagogue, the Charlottesville riot which joined racist and anti-Semitic rhetoric and action.

. . .

Bessie and Philip left Philadelphia and moved to a suburb just west of the city limits. The 1930 census records the family residence in Ardmore. By now they were a family of five: my uncle Bernard, known as Bern, born 1918, originally named Israel but renamed Bernard because a markedly Jewish name like Israel would brand him as an outcast. Next came my uncle Julius, born in 1923, and my mother Gertrude, known as Trudy, born in 1928.

During the periods of the twenties, thirties, and forties I know little of the details of my grandmother and her life. I know little of the details of my mother and her life. That is the way of children: for many years they do not know or care that their parents and grandparents had lives before they were born. By the time they do care, anyone who could or would talk about their lives and their stories is gone.

The thirties and forties were bleak and terrifying years.

First came the Great Depression. Summer nights were spent sleeping on the fire escape, wrapped in sheets drenched in ice water against the blistering heat. My grandmother took in mending and alterations to help make ends meet and feed her family. Food and money were scarce. My grandmother did the best she could to stretch a meal of noodles and cottage cheese to feed five people. Still, everyone was always hungry.

. . .

My grandfather was a furrier to wealthy families who lived

in grand Tudor estates on the Main Line. My mother used to accompany him, dreaming of a room of her own in a beautifully appointed house with a white cloth-covered table laid with crystal and silver. When the foreign-sounding furrier and his young daughter arrived to deliver the heavy mink coats made by hand, they were told to come to the back door, whether because they were poor, or Jewish, or spoke with a foreign accent like my grandfather, I don't know. My mother, ashamed of her homemade clothes, longing for store-bought dresses from Strawbridge's like those worn by her classmates. My mother was ashamed of her immigrant parents, their fractured English and the tiny apartment with a bedroom she shared with her two brothers.

The back door was for those who weren't good enough to go through the front door.

My mother spent weekends at the Ardmore Free Public Library, a fieldstone building facing a beautiful fountain. Books were free and books were freedom. A book could come home with my mother and stay for a while like a good friend. My mother didn't have many friends; she was a lonely child, and books kept her company.

• • •

In the beginning my grandmother tried to hold on to the traditions she'd grown up with. She kept a kosher home. She lit the Friday night Sabbath candles.

My grandmother would not have known how to pray in Hebrew. Such learning was reserved for men. She may have recited a *tekhine,* a private prayer in Yiddish. She may have asked the Holy One's blessing on her home and family. I imagine her standing in front of a small table with a white cloth, perhaps brass candlesticks, she could not have afforded silver. Her back is to me. I cannot see her face as she circles her hands above the candles' dancing flames to welcome the Sabbath.

One day, my mother told me, she came home from school and found a carp in the bathtub. My grandmother had taken the train from Ardmore to Philadelphia to buy it so she could make gefilte fish.

Carp vary anywhere in length from 16 inches to 31 inches. Was the carp my mother found dead or alive? If it was dead, what was it doing in the bathtub? And if it was alive, was my grandmother, who barely reached five feet (she was tall in inner strength but short in stature) really prepared to flay it? And how would she have carried a live carp home from Philly on a train? In a huge plastic bag, as if it were a humongous prize goldfish won at the county fair?

Eventually the rituals and traditions from her past became burdensome obstacles to the all-encompassing goal of assimilation. The ethos of the time was the melting pot; immigrants were expected to lose their foreignness and become true Americans. Any outward signs that accentuated difference – foreign names, strange traditions, heavy accents, unusual clothing – blocked the way to acceptance, to becoming American. My grandparents never lost their accents and were always outsiders.

They did not blend in. They had few friends.

They must have lived a very lonely, isolated life.

• • •

Then came the Second World War. My mother and her classmates spent their school days knitting socks and scarves for the boys shipping off to Europe and the South Pacific. Everyone supported the war effort, especially American soldiers who gave their lives to the cause. Everyone was on the side of good against evil.

My mother's oldest brother Bern served as an army medic. My uncle Julius, shy and sensitive at the age of 18, was sent to the brutal arenas of Italy and North Africa where he saw heavy combat. He returned with a bronze star, a purple heart, and a case of PTSD so profound that it lasted the rest of his life, which he took at the age of 60 in the bathroom of my grandmother's house.

. . .

Sometime after the war, maybe during the late forties or early fifties, my grandmother and grandfather bought a semi-detached gray fieldstone house on Chatham Road, a quiet side street in Ardmore just off the Main Line. Perhaps my uncle Bern, now a doctor—after the war, educational opportunities opened for returning military personnel—gave them the money to do so. My mother and uncle Julius went to live there too; my uncle Bern was married and lived in New Jersey with his wife and their young sons.

The fieldstone house on Chatham Road is where I see my grandmother in my mind's eye. I knew that house; I often stayed there. I see her bending toward her vast collection of plants lining the front and side balustrades of the front porch, watering the spiky dracaena, red coleus, dark ferns and pale spiders.

I see her hunched on the tired gray sofa in the living room, her mouth puckered in concentration as she draws her needle in and out to hem my new skirt.

I see her in the kitchen. My grandmother is always the first to awaken. I've been lured downstairs by the caramelized aroma of burnt toast. My grandmother always burned the toast. After a few years the toaster stopped working and burned everything: bagels, bialys and bread, but my frugal grandmother refuses to replace this appliance. She also refuses to toss away the burnt toast, memories of hunger still burning in her mind. We eat the dark brown toast with the singed crusts. If you slather it with butter and jam it isn't too bad.

I see myself standing at the kitchen doorway, gazing at my grandmother as she sits facing the window, a plate of burnt toast and a cup of hot tea with lemon on the table before her. The kitchen walls are painted a pale yellow and the room is bathed in the soft yellow light of an early morning glow. My grandmother is staring out the window. It's a tall window with a yellow-and-white checkered valance and a few green plants on the sill. I imagine she doesn't know I'm there but that's a trick of memory. My grandmother's senses are sharp and she has heard me come down the stairs but hasn't yet turned to greet me.

In the brief silence I try to imagine her thoughts. Are they occupied with meal preparations, alterations of skirts I've brought from home, the day's ironing and vacuuming? I wonder now whether we'd turned my grandmother into a servant or whether these chores gave her comfort, kept her mind occupied and protected from thoughts about the mother she'd left behind in Russia, the grown son who lived with her and never married, the daughter, my mother, who was always irritable and impatient with her.

I enter the kitchen and take a seat caddy-corner to my grandmother on a chair covered with red vinyl that's starting to crack. My grandmother gives me a small smile. Her welcome is not in the lift of her mouth but in her blue-gray eyes, which become brighter. In a flash she is upright, moving swiftly back and forth between counter and stove, setting another place, pouring me a glass of orange juice. "Nency," she says, "would you like some toast?"

• • •

I see my grandmother standing at the counter in my mother's kitchen with its honey-colored pine cabinets. She wears an apron over her printed dress and announces she will bake an apple pie. My grandmother's hands are quick as she begins to assemble a mound from flour, sugar, eggs and butter. The dough is sticky and I try to help her shape it, but it glues to my fingers. I don't like the stickiness on my hands; I'd rather watch. But first we must gather the apples.

There is an enormous apple tree in our backyard, and every autumn my brother and I are summoned by my father to gather apples that have fallen and collect them in bags for the town's compost pile. I hate this task of bending and picking up the apples. It's tedious, tiring, and endless. Sometimes from boredom and irritation I roll the apples down the small hill into our neighbor's yard. They too have a large apple tree; how will they ever know which apples are theirs and which are ours? But when my grandmother bustles into the house armed with grocery bags, I hurry outside to pick the ripe apples, cradling them in my palm to make sure they are smooth and unbruised, knowing I will reap the fruits of my labor when that pie, simmering, fragrant with cinnamon and sweetness, is lifted from the oven.

My grandmother slices the apples with a knife she complains is not sharp enough. Her slices are thin, even, and perfect, not like the chunks I cut when I want a snack. Her pie is a work of art.

• • •

My grandmother and I are rushing through the industrial halls of Philadelphia's cavernous Suburban Station, trying to catch the train that will take us back to Ardmore after a shopping excursion to Wanamaker's downtown flagship department store. My grandmother is always rushing, I can barely keep up with her even though I am nine years old and she is very, very old (even though she was about 65, the same age I am now).

My grandmother was always old, her face creased and tired. Her features are sad and faded, like a sepia photograph exposed too long to the light. But even so, in spite of her careworn expression, she is always in a hurry, maybe in an effort to recapture what she has lost.

We're in Suburban Station looking for the platform and my grandmother can't read. I am frightened by the crowds pressing up against us and the thick, dense air pushing us along like a strong gust of wind, by the heavy steel beams overhead that may fall on our heads and squash us as though we are bugs. I can read but my grandmother doesn't want me to help, even though I ask her, *Should we go to the Information Center, it's just over there.* She is the grown-up; she wants to be in charge. At last, she sees it, the number nine, a dark black mark on a white metal sign hanging from a column. It seems she has taught herself to recognize numbers. Her sigh is audible; intangible particles start lifting around us, leaving room for me to breathe. My stomach unknots, my hands unclench. Together we board the train.

Nency, my grandmother says, searching her pocketbook for our tickets as she shifts the Wanamaker's bag on her lap, *vat do you vant for dinner?*

We aren't lost, and we're not falling through a black hole in the universe. My grandmother has rescued us. Soon we'll be home.

· · ·

At my grandmother's house I sleep in a bedroom that once belonged to my mother. Next door is my uncle Julius's room. Down the hall there's a bathroom, and at the far end of the hall a bedroom that belongs to my grandparents, which is where my parents sleep when we visit. My grandparents sleep on the pull-out sofa downstairs in the living room.

The headboard of my mother's bed is made of reddish-brown maple. There is a matching dresser against the wall between two windows, facing the back of the house. If you part the dotted Swiss curtains and look outside, you'll see a concrete walkway that runs parallel to the entire length of the street; this path behind the row of houses is where kids hang out and homeowners place their trash cans. The walkway is bordered by a chain-link fence that guards a small, wooded area between Chatham Road and the next street.

My brother sleeps on a narrow cot. No one, least of all me, questions this arrangement. I am older and I'm the only girl among my grandmother's four grandchildren. Naturally I sleep in my mother's bed.

Of my own accord I went to sleep early in those days. My parents didn't object, they were probably only too happy to be relieved of the watchful tensions of parenting. I'd lie on my back in my mother's bed and gaze at the ceiling, watching blue light fill the room. I'd listen to kids laughing and shouting, the incessant whirring of cicadas and crickets, and the clacking of train wheels on the nearby tracks. I was shy, and I had no wish to be running around with the neighborhood kids whom I didn't know, who had grown up together. I'd review the day's events, turning them over and over in my mind the way one inspects interesting shells or smooth stones found on the beach. I tried to create a story about whatever the day had brought – a walk to the park, a talk with my grandmother on the front porch, a car ride for ice cream—butter pecan or mint chocolate chip. It was an impossible choice because I wanted both, I always wanted everything all at once. I was greedy, hungry for approval and affection that felt unavailable to me from my mother. I felt at home when I was with my grandmother. Even then, I wanted more from her, I could never get enough.

• • •

I didn't get along with my mother. She was distant, unaffectionate.

My mother didn't get along with her mother. My mother was snippy and impatient with her. I got on very well with my grandmother. My mother must have felt jealous and excluded.

My grandmother called me *shayne maidele*, her pretty girl.

When I was nine, I asked my mother if I was pretty. She thought for a moment and said I was cute. I remember her hesitation, those begrudging words. Cute, but not pretty. Babies are cute. Puppies are cute. Girls on the verge of adolescence don't want to be cute. They want to be pretty.

Maybe my mother's mother had said those very same words to her.

• • •

I experienced more freedom at my grandmother's than I did at home with my mother. For all her many anxieties, my grandmother did not fret if I walked alone to the bookstore in Suburban Square, about 15 minutes on foot.

When I was grown, my mother told me that on the rare occasions she'd let me walk home from school instead of taking the school bus, she'd follow me in her car to make sure I was safe. I never knew she'd done such a thing. Had her mother been frantic about her when she was a child?

Even though I hadn't realized my mother was following me, I knew she obsessively worried about me. I was not allowed to play anywhere except in our front yard or across the street at the neighbor's house, where luckily there lived a girl the same age as me.

● ● ●

The walk to the Suburban Square bookstore was a great adventure. I paid close attention to the crosswalk signal the way I'd been taught, then traversed Lancaster Avenue, a crowded four-lane thoroughfare that linked Philadelphia to the suburbs. A side street took me across an arched concrete bridge that crossed high above the railroad tracks and led to another street, shaded and quiet, which eventually opened onto the square with its corner bookstore.

This tree-lined street was empty, there were never any children about, and I held my breath as I rushed past shuttered-looking houses that felt full of menace and reminded me of Boo Radley's place in *To Kill a Mockingbird.* Then suddenly I emerged into sunlight and the bustling, open square filled with shoppers.

At the bookstore there was a revolving rack with Signet paperbacks. I was drawn to the colorful covers, violet, maple, ochre, sage. My grandmother had given me a quarter, and for twenty-five cents I could own a copy of John Steinbeck's *The Red Pony* or Gilbreth's *Cheaper by the Dozen* or Frances Hodgson Burnett's *The Little Princess.* And these books, beautiful and desirable as miniature paintings, belonged to me alone. Unlike volumes borrowed from the library, I could possess these treasures forever. I didn't have to share them with anyone. From a very young age I did not like to share, perhaps because what I really wanted--my mother's affection--was so out of reach.

● ● ●

In my collection of family photographs there's a photo of my grandmother at the beach with my grandfather and their three children. My mother looks to be five years old, so Julius would have been ten and Bern fifteen. My grandparents flank their kids like bookends. Standing between them are the children in column fashion: Bern behind Julius, his hands on his younger brother's shoulders, and Julius behind my mother. The boys and their father wear dark tank swimsuits, as was the custom for males at that time.

This was 1933, the height of the Great Depression. Perhaps the family took the train for a day's escape to Atlantic City, a bustling resort town known for its wide beaches and famous boardwalk where open-air shops with striped awnings sold cotton candy and saltwater taffy. Perhaps Bessie packed a picnic basket with sandwiches and soda pop. Bern and Julius would have carried blankets and towels coiled under their arms like swiss cake rolls.

I study their expressions. Bern looks pleased, he is the firstborn and a son to boot. Intelligent, a good student, his success will repair the shame of this family's financial struggles and immigrant roots. My grandfather looks tired, he's responsible for providing for the family; even a day at the beach doesn't diminish his burden. Julius wears a begrudging grin, *smile for the camera* they'd told him, but he'd rather be splashing in the waves instead of standing here in the sweltering sun waiting for the snap of the shutter. My mother, the youngest, the only girl, squints against the brightness, her face an unwritten story. And my grandmother, hands on hips, smiles as though she is enjoying the day. Yet there's something troubled about her gaze which is distant and distracted, as if she's not truly in her body, as though her mind has gone somewhere else, into the secret sadness of her past.

• • •

My grandmother raised three troubled children. My uncle Bern was a devoted husband and father, but he had terrible relationships with my mother and Julius. Bern and my mother barely spoke to each other; he treated my mother and Julius with a coldness that bordered on cruelty. He could become very angry, his face turning crimson, his voice like the smack of thunder. My mother was afraid of his temper, as was my grandmother.

My mother suffered from a serious depression before drugs like Prozac were available. Her moods ranged from despondency to total meltdowns. She would explode over what to me seemed the simplest things – overcooking the roast beef, circling for a parking spot, misplacing her keys. I was afraid of her rages, which were sometimes directed at me.

My uncle Julius also suffered from major depression which grew worse and worse over time. In the late 1970s he was hospitalized and received electroconvulsive shock treatments intended to alleviate his suffering. The electroshock treatments did not work.

In 1983 Julius was living alone in the house on Chatham Road. My grandmother had moved to a facility for senior citizens about 20 minutes away, just inside the Philadelphia city limits. One evening he went to the pink-and-black tiled bathroom down the hall from his bedroom, swallowed most of a bottle of vodka along with nearly all his medication, and left a note saying he was very sorry, he just couldn't stand the pain anymore. His body was discovered when the neighbor on the other side of the semi-detached house began to smell a foul odor seeping through the wall adjoining the two houses.

His death came as a terrible shock. I remember sitting on the sofa in the living room of my grandmother's house on Chatham Road; my parents and I had driven straight to Ardmore after we received the phone call. The atmosphere was suffocating, a miasma of anguish and grief. I thought I might faint.

My uncle Bern was enraged. Julius had not included Bern's two sons in his will. He left his estate to my grandmother, with any proceeds following her death to be divided between me and my brother. He appointed Bern as the executor of his will.

Julius loved my brother and me, but he created a mess by excluding Bern's sons. Bern accused my father of influencing Julius but I could tell by my father's face that he was surprised, taken aback by what Julius had done. At the time I assumed Julius left the estate in trust to my brother and me because we were his surrogate children. Now I think he also wished to hurt his brother. I'm not sure why.

I don't remember where my grandmother was that terrible day. She had probably taken to bed with a sedative, perhaps administered by her son the doctor.

• • •

I'd had no quarrel with my uncle Bern before Julius's death. We were never close, not connected the way I was to Julius, but Bern had always been friendly to me.

After Julius's death, that changed. He was cold and distant. I was a reminder of what his brother had done. By cutting Bern's children out of the will, he had cut off Bern too. Except he'd made him executor, inflaming Bern's anger and resentment.

It was a mess, an example of how family members can turn against each other and cause tension and friction, even after they're gone.

As one of my cousins said to me, "Death doesn't solve anything."

• • •

We are gathered at the table for Thanksgiving in my grandmother's modest dining room.

There's something almost sacred about the Thanksgiving table, the ritual of sitting together at a beautifully laid table. And my grandmother has set a beautiful table: a white linen cloth she's embroidered with clusters of purple and yellow flowers, along with china, gleaming flatware, cut glass goblets, and a pair of white tapered candles throwing their light toward the chandelier with its dangles of glass crystals. There's money now: my uncle, who lives at home, is working; Bern is working; poverty belongs to the past.

My grandmother has prepared a feast: an enormous roast turkey, sweet potato casserole topped with a layer of caramelized marshmallows, homemade stuffing and cranberry sauce, green beans. "Ma, you've outdone yourself," my father says.

My grandmother barely acknowledges this praise as she bustles back and forth between the kitchen and our table. She refuses our help, even though it's clear she is tired.

What keeps her going? How does she manage in the face of such fatigue?

By the time dessert is served she's exhausted. My mother and I, and my Aunt Selma, Bern's wife, are finally allowed to pitch in and relieve her as she collapses in her chair at the end of the table, which has been empty almost the entire meal.

We sat together at the table, a rare occasion, without bickering. After dessert my uncle and his sons move to the living room, where they can watch the football game on tv.

For now, we are a family.

• • •

My grandfather Philip is a shadowy figure. He was quiet, a good-natured man who wore a gentle smile and round gold-wire spectacles. I imagine he must have been somewhat passive to withstand my grandmother and the whirlwind force of her will.

I have few memories of Philip. I remember sitting on his lap in the French reproduction fauteuil in my mother's living room, where he would tickle me by running his finger along my spine or clucking my ribs. This is the only interaction I can recall. In this memory there is no speech, just Philip's lap and my ticklish laughter.

When I was ten Philip and Bessie were staying with us. They used to babysit from time to time when my parents went away. Philip had taken his Rambler to the grocery store and on the way home his car struck a kid speeding down River Vale Road on a bicycle. The boy fell off his bike and ended up in the hospital with a broken leg. The accident shook Philip to his core, and he never drove again.

Though the boy mercifully recovered, Philip began to decline. Dementia lodged itself in his brain and at night he'd open the front door of the house on Chatham Road and wander the streets. My grandmother would awaken to find an empty space beside her and rush outside in her nightgown with a flashlight, frantically calling his name in the midnight darkness. Eventually she could no longer care for him, and he went to live in a nursing home.

My grandmother was sick with guilt over what she'd done; in the Old Country the elderly and infirm lived and died at home with family; sending a husband to an institution was unheard of. The lines on her face deepened and she'd shake with anguished weeping.

But there was no other choice. Philip had become a danger to himself, and his night wanderings were wearing my 73-year-old grandmother to the bone.

He died in 1968 when I was twelve. I was not permitted to go to the funeral; my mother thought I'd find it too upsetting.

What my mother didn't realize was that children need to be

included in mourning rituals as well as celebrations. Watching my mother shuffle through the house clutching her hair and sobbing was profoundly disturbing, since I had no real context for understanding what was happening to her. Philip's death felt abstract and unreal. What was death, anyway? What had happened to my grandfather, where had he gone? When was he coming back? Why wouldn't anyone talk to me about him?

• • •

My grandmother lived almost 20 years following the death of her husband, four of those years following the death of her son. She passed away of congestive heart failure in 1987, when she was 92.

I think she would have lived longer had Julius not taken his life.

At his funeral she tried to throw herself into the open wound of his grave, lurching toward the lowered coffin as if she wanted to join her son and sleep in the darkness that was about to swallow him forever. It took two men, my father and my uncle Bern, to restrain her.

• • •

My brother and I are walking to the park, ten minutes or so on foot from my grandmother's house. I am ten years old and my brother is three years younger. I've been given a great responsibility to watch over my him, and it's difficult for me to keep from bossing him around, to keep from treating him the way I feel treated by my mother.

I am jealous of him. He is cooperative and easy to get along with; he is said to take after our grandfather Philip. I am moody and stubborn. Who do I take after?

We are carrying wooden tennis rackets tucked beneath our arms; I also carry a canvas tote with a can of tennis balls and a book. I feel rather smug about the rackets; they make us acceptable in this place with its fieldstone churches and Welsh pedigree, towns with names like Bryn Mawr and Bala Cynwyd. At school a few boys make fun of me because I'm Jewish. I am the only Jewish kid in my class. But here, no one knows about our hideousness, the ugliness of our Jewish souls. We look like respectable children strolling along in our white shorts and white shirts to a country club that's restricted. No Jews allowed.

When we arrive at the park, we head for the practice area where we bounce the ball on the macadam and hit it against the wall. There are also clay courts here, and sometimes our father, an avid player, will find pick-up games. But today it's just my brother and me.

After hitting the tennis ball against the wall five times I sit myself down on the grass and pick up my book. My brother is more interested in physical activity than I am. I have no patience for tennis or anything that involves running after a ball. I'd much rather immerse myself in a good story. From time to time I look up as he chases the ball back and forth. I lob a few encouraging words his way. *Good job, Larr!"*

In another area of the park is a playground with an enormous concrete turtle sitting inside a sandbox. This turtle has many carved niches where children can place their sneakers as they clamber up its gigantic shell. The turtle is so big that several children can be climbing at once. I have climbed up this turtle many times when I was younger, but now I am too grown up for such games. I think about the turtle and wish I were clambering about on its back.

• • •

My uncle Julius worked as an accountant for the state's Civil Service. Photographs of him as a young man portray him as quite handsome, with sharp, well-defined features. I never knew his good looks. In my earliest memories of him he was in his forties, his face softened, sad and avuncular, the good looking features swallowed by weight gain and depression.

My father told me that when Julius was approaching forty, he was engaged to a woman my parents liked very much, a warm woman my parents thought would be a loving, stable match. This woman, though, had serious doubts about Julius's mental health. My father said he talked with her at length and tried to reassure her, but the woman backed away and broke off the engagement. And so my uncle's future as a husband and father vanished. Julius lost hope, and his depression worsened.

My uncle's bedroom on Chatham Road was adjacent to where I slept. If I woke up in the middle of the night to go to the bathroom down the hall, I would pass his room and hear groaning and thrashing. During the day the door to his room was sometimes left ajar, and just visible through the doorway was a depression in the wall alongside his bed the size of a man's fist. Yes, my mother told me, Julius had punched a hole in the wall while he slept, probably from nightmares of the battle-torn war years that continued to haunt him.

Julius never had children; my brother and I were his surrogate kids. He took us to an amusement park where I rode the one and only roller coaster of my life and proceeded to vomit all over the pavement as soon as I got off. He took us to Valley Forge National Historical Park, the site of George Washington's winter encampment of 1778, where I tried to imagine the vast, empty greensward filled with ragged soldiers huddled in tents against the freezing gale winds. He took us to the playground in Narberth where I sat on a small metal horse atop a coiled spring that rocked back and forth, back and forth. He took us to the diner where we sat at the counter and ordered grilled cheese sandwiches and egg creams as I twirled around on the revolving stool, something I never did with my parents who always insisted on sitting in a booth.

Before his retirement he enjoyed a day at the racetrack and traveling on group tours to Europe. He always brought me back a doll. For many years I kept them. I loved dolls and collected them; the dolls he gave me were beautifully dressed in the colors of their country – a Spanish señorita in red with a black lace mantilla, a Dutch milkmaid in a blue smock, yellow ribbons dangling from her bonnet.

He retired when he was in his early fifties, much to my parents' consternation. They were right; the lack of structure and social isolation increased his loneliness, and his depression deepened.

• • •

On my grandmother's front porch there's a set of furniture coated in white powder aluminum: a double glider with green-and-white striped cushions, a rocker, and a chair. The glider is my favorite since you can slide back and forth. But my grandmother has taken the chair and, in order to be close to her, I take the rocker which is separated from her by a small white aluminum table. My grandmother is crocheting a blue-and-white afghan for my bedroom at home. The coleus, ferns, and ivy in their yellow and teal ceramic pots keep us company.

As my grandmother captures the yarn on her crochet hook she answers my flow of questions about our extended family. Her fingers know crochet so well she doesn't need to keep too close an eye on her work, not the way she does with hemming and embroidery. Just by feeling the tension as she hooks the yarn she can tell whether or not she's made a mistake, which she rarely does.

The topic of family is endlessly fascinating to me. I don't understand how I am related to so many people I barely know. Why is it no one speaks to each other? Where has everyone gone?

My grandmother had four siblings: Ida, Ensa, Joe, and Elick. My grandmother's brother Elick died in 1962 when I was six; I have no memory of him. In my uncle's genealogical record there are no dates of birth or death for Ida, Ensa, and Joe.

My grandfather Philip also had four siblings: Rose, Max, Joe, and Israel. Joe and Israel died in the early 1960s, I have no memory of them, and there are no dates recording the births and deaths of Rose and Max.

I sit in the rocker on the front porch while my grandmother talks about these people, her brothers and sisters, Philip's brothers and sisters. How they made a living, who they were married to. Their children and grandchildren, the second cousins I don't know. I've met my cousin Everett, Lillian's son, who is a year older than I am. He and I play tag in his driveway.

My grandmother becomes exasperated with me because when she gets to the end of the story, I ask her to start again.

When I review the genealogy reconstructed by my uncle Bern I don't see Lillian or Everett listed anywhere. And yet I know my mother was fond of Lillian; she used to speak of Lillian with warmth and affection. Lillian, whose thick hair and glasses reminded me of my mother.

When my grandmother told me the stories of her siblings and Philip's I never really paid attention to the details. What I liked was the sound of her voice weaving a yarn about the people who made up her world. I did not know most of them. They were no more than shadows and ghosts to me.

My extended family was and will always be a mystery. I've lost contact with every one of my cousins. Old grudges, resentments and anger die hard. Competition for scarce financial resources. Who snubbed whom. Who was generous with gifts and who wasn't. Who never telephoned, never visited, never wrote a thank-you note.

When my mother passed away in 2016 several close friends came to pay their respects at her funeral, but there was not a single person, not one, from her large extended family. She had lost touch with them, and they had lost touch with her.

• • •

I'm sitting on the front porch with my grandmother with a basket of yarn at my feet. I've asked her to teach me to knit.

She has already taught me crochet and embroidery. Crochet is boring with its one hook endlessly looping along, but I love to embroider. I've mastered the chain stitch, split stitch, and many others, including French knots which are challenging if you don't maintain the correct tension as you wrap the floss around the needle. When successful, French knots are lovely, little bouquets of color smile brightly from the cloth.

Knitting is another story.

For some reason, I seem to have no dexterity in my left hand and cannot get the needle to cooperate. My right hand, which I use for crochet and embroidery, works quite well but this left one keeps making mistakes, won't hold the tension of the yarn, keeps slipping. My grandmother and I laugh ruefully as the scarf I'm working on becomes more and more lopsided and misshapen.

Finally I give up, fed up with this disaster. My grandmother sighs with relief. So I won't be a knitter like my grandmother. At least I have embroidery.

‎• • •

In 1980 my grandmother went to live in a senior citizens home just inside the Philadelphia city limits. It was a depressing place, a large, impersonal apartment-like building facing a wide driveway that circled underneath a covered portico. There had been a series of ugly arguments between Julius, my mother, and my uncle Bern about who was responsible for my grandmother. Julius said he bore most of the burden since he lived with her. Eventually the siblings agreed that my grandmother, who was 85, should move to a facility where she would receive better care. What that meant I'm not sure. There may have been a nurse on staff who would check on the residents from time to time. I never saw one.

My grandmother could no longer bustle about from task to task but she was not ill, not as far as I knew. Perhaps Julius was angry that she was emotionally dependent on him, or resentful of his siblings and their independent lives. My grandmother was very unhappy about going into the home, at being farmed out of her house.

I don't have the moral authority to judge my mother and my uncles. I helped farm my mother out of her house when we were told she needed more medical care. The choices of how to help elderly parents are not always clear, and sometimes no matter what choice you make, your heart will be broken.

Julius may have imagined he would fare better without the responsibility of caring for my grandmother, but he was sadly mistaken. Within three years of her departure from the house he took his life. Perhaps out of loneliness, perhaps out of guilt, who can say?

Perhaps he realized he loved his mother more than he'd known. Perhaps he missed her. Perhaps he was too ashamed to ask her to come back when he understood he couldn't live alone.

• • •

In the late 1970s I was an undergrad at University of Pennsylvania in Philadelphia. In those days my grandmother was still living with my uncle Julius in the house on Chatham Road. To visit them I walked seven long blocks to 30th Street Station and took the train to Ardmore, walked a few short blocks from the station and there I was, at the fieldstone house. My grandmother had prepared dinner – something simple like meatloaf and baked potatoes—and the three of us would sit at the kitchen table.

These meals were dreadfully uncomfortable.

My uncle had been become very depressed. The heavy fog of despair was written in the shadows on his face, in his shuttered eyes. My grandmother was also suffering. Her blue-gray eyes seemed to sink into her face; sadness etched long lines down her cheeks. Looking back, I imagine the discussions of what would happen to her in view of my uncle's wish to send her to a home had already begun. But I didn't know this at the time.

We ate in silence. I tried to amuse them with small talk about my classes and my roommates, the time we wanted chocolate sundaes but had no ice cream so we melted Hershey bars from the hall vending machine on our stovetop and ate the sauce right from the pan. My grandmother and uncle tried to smile, tried to look amused, but I had failed. The corners of their mouths lifted slightly but their eyes remained dead and lifeless.

My uncle drove me back to school after dinner. The darkness inside the car was denser and more impenetrable than the starless night outside the car doors. We drove without speaking. The only words that passed between us, when he pulled up in front of my dorm, were, "Good to see you. See you soon."

There was so much I wanted to say but the words were glued inside my throat.

What's happening to you?
Where have you gone?
What can I do?

I was twenty years old, barely out of my teens. I could not bring myself to ask my uncle these questions, for which there were no answers.

. . .

The senior citizen's home where my grandmother lived was 20 or so stories tall, a brutal brick building. This was in the days before assisted living facilities, which are also institutional in character but at least gesture toward residents' comfort. At the home there was no common room; residents sat in chairs against the gray walls of the lobby as they waited for visitors or the next meal.

My stomach always clenched as we passed through the revolving doors and entered the building. I felt the impersonality of the place hit me like a blast of frigid air. I missed the fieldstone house on Chatham Road; I missed my grandmother's presence there.

This place reminded me of a warehouse.

My grandmother's apartment was a cramped studio, her bed screened off from the kitchenette/living room by a bookcase maybe six feet high.

When we came to visit my mother would come laden with bags filled with foods for our lunch: bagels, tuna and egg salads, whitefish, lox, plates of fruit, boxes of cookies, maybe a cake.

There was barely room on the table for everything my mother had brought. There was barely room at the table for the four of us to squeeze together (I believe my brother wasn't with us because he was in college). I could feel the tension in the air: my grandmother's loneliness; my mother's attempts to assuage her sense of guilt by feeding her mother; my own sadness at seeing my grandmother so diminished, stripped of her dignity as queen of the household.

These visits depleted everyone. After lunch my grandmother lay down on her bed, my father stretched out on the couch, and my mother and I slumped in the two armchairs brought from Chatham Road. Each of us had a headache.

• • •

My father was very fond of my grandmother, even though she still distrusted him thirty-five years after she'd first met him. He came from an affluent, educated family; she worried he would look down on her. He did not – he had lost his mother when he was twelve years old to mental illness and a raging infection she'd contacted in a sanitarium. My grandmother was his surrogate mother, suspicious of him as she was because he'd taken her daughter away from her to the wilds of northern New Jersey. My mother was the only one of my grandmother's children to move away; Julius never left home, and my uncle Bern lived outside Camden, maybe thirty minutes from the house on Chatham Road.

I can only imagine what it was like for my grandmother to feel she had lost her daughter. She'd already lost her mother; she wanted her daughter close by.

Leaving home must have been the most traumatic event she could imagine.

• • •

When we'd go to dinner there was always an argument between my father and my grandmother about who would pay the check.

I remember a meal at a locally famous Jewish deli, near the city line. Those were the days when you could eat corned beef or pastrami on rye and not even think about cholesterol.

After the waiter took our order, my grandmother turned to him and said she wanted to pay the check.

Shortly after this my father excused himself. He went to find the waiter and told him he wanted to pay the check.

When the meal ended and the waiter arrived with the check, there was a flailing about and attempts by my father and grandmother to grab the check from the waiter, who ended up tossing it in the middle of the table in exasperation.

I don't remember who ended up paying the check.

• • •

When I was in my 20's I became engaged to my college sweetheart, who was enrolled in a doctoral program in economics at Columbia University.

When I told my grandmother about the engagement, she wanted to know about my fiancé, what did he do for a living? When I told her about the doctorate, she recognized the word doctor, and, at the same time, intuited he would not be a physician like my Uncle Bern.

"But he's not a real doctor," she said. "Will he make a living?"

"He'll teach," I said. "Don't worry, we'll be fine."

My grandmother came to our wedding, a strained expression of worry and anxiety masking her face as she walked down the aisle in a sparkly, sequined dress she hadn't worn in many years.

Julius was there, too, in a powder blue suit, looking as if the lifeblood was draining out of him.

In less than two years he'd be gone.

• • •

After the wedding I decided to take Yiddish classes at a local synagogue. I wanted to speak to my grandmother in her mother tongue; I wanted to honor the legacy of Yiddish, which was disappearing as a spoken language except among Hasidic Jews.

There were three people in the class: my husband and I, and another student.

After a few lessons I called my grandmother on the telephone. By this time, she was very hard of hearing.

"Grandmom," I shouted into the phone. "*Vos makst tu*?" How are you?

"Nency," my grandmother shouted back. "Vat are you saying? I ken't understand you!"`

Shortly after that I dropped the class.

• • •

Silence, the response of people who've survived trauma.

My grandmother, the traumatic loss of her home and her mother. The complete and irreversible severing of contact. My grandmother could not write, so she couldn't write letters. My great-grandmother probably couldn't read. By the time my grandmother had a telephone, who knows if anyone was alive in Russia to answer it.

Anti-Semitism. My grandparents knew it and fled it. But they found it in the New World in a different guise. Not the threat of death. But:

isolation
friendlessness
the desperate attempt to be accepted
the discarding of traditions
the erasure of names
the shame of revealing one's origins.

So much loss must be acknowledged.

Must be mourned and witnessed by the larger culture.

But was not.

• • •

My uncle Julius. The spilling of blood across the battlefields of Europe. The inability to talk about what he saw. World War II was the good war, the righteous war.

To reveal his shellshock, his trauma, would have been unmanly.

A sign of weakness.

Unpatriotic.

The diagnosis of post-traumatic stress disorder did not come into use until the 1970s, in response to the extreme trauma of Vietnam veterans. It was not added to the Diagnostic Statistical Manual, the psychiatric bible of diagnoses, until 1980.

Before then, the condition was known as shellshock. This is what my mother called it.

She knew her brother had been severely damaged by the war.

The term shellshock implies a kind of physicality, a visceral response to shelling and other sensory stimuli.

Traditionally, it has been more acceptable to recognize physical trauma than emotional and psychic trauma. To recognize the latter implies that soldiers are capable of empathy, not just for their fellow combatants but also for the enemy.

If we recognize the humanity of the enemy, we might begin to question our justifications for war.

And then where would we be?

• • •

Somewhere in Ekaterinaslav a woman in a kerchief sits at a

table and weeps.

Her children are gone, all five of them. This last one was the hardest to let go of. Her *tokhter*, her daughter, the youngest. The baby of the family.

What is the name for a woman who has lost all her children?

The city is quieter, the Jewish quarter emptied of young people. No shouting and laughing in the streets. No visits to the matchmaker. No gossiping with the other mothers.

The women who've lost their children keep to themselves.

She is no longer young. This last one, the girl who just left, came as a surprise; she thought she could no longer bear children.

She hopes her own days are numbered. The pain is too much to bear.

My mother never knew her grandparents. All four lived in the Pale of Settlement. She never met them, never spoke to them, never received any letters from them.

Perhaps she never heard about them because she knew enough not to ask questions.

• • •

Several years ago I was invited by a colleague to speak to her college English class.

I read from a chapbook of poems I had written about my father, a refugee from Nazi Germany.

The students were interested, sympathetic. Most were immigrants or children of immigrants who had fled poverty and political violence in Central America. Some ran from the turmoil in Syria and other Middle Eastern nations. They identified with my father's story.

That day I read a poem I'd written, entitled, "We Are All Refugees."

I told the students that as a white woman who had grown up in middle class privilege I wasn't sure I should write a poem with that title. They told me they liked the poem. I felt buoyed and encouraged by their validation.

We talked about becoming American. Those of us who come from another place, or with parents or grandparents who come from another place, often feel we have one foot in a different world, a world whose language and traditions we are asked to give up, erase, forget. It can feel like a terrible loss, as though we've lost part of ourselves and our history.

And yet often we can't really give a name to what we've lost. We feel the losses experienced by our parents or grandparents. It's not our loss, and yet it is.

And then we are not able to speak freely of these losses, as though to do so would somehow mean we're ungrateful for the opportunities afforded us in this country. As though to do so would be a betrayal.

And so we bury these feelings, these losses, the ghosts of those left behind.

But they are always with us.

Sometimes I feel I'm in exile, a refugee.

• • •

When my grandmother passed away in 1987 from congestive heart failure I asked to speak at her funeral.

It was the first time I'd given a eulogy, and I didn't know how difficult it is to talk spontaneously, meaningfully, and coherently when one is grieving. I hadn't prepared any remarks in advance, hoping my thoughts would just flow. But instead of flowing, I found myself stumbling; without a narrative, without the right words I could not convey who my grandmother was: a strong woman, a woman who'd survived the loss of her mother, her home, and her mother tongue; who raised a family under grinding conditions of poverty and anti-Semitism; a woman who loved me and whom I loved deeply.

A woman I admired, who taught me about perseverance. A woman with a sense of humor. Who spoke to me in snippets of Yiddish. Who called me her *shayne maidele*.

Zei gezunt, Grandmom. Go in good health.

Farewell.

I didn't have the right words at her burial to tell the story of my grandmother.

But I do now.

# # #

We Are All Refugees

We are all refugees.
For who are we
if not seekers
of asylum
from the ghosts
of our past?
We all need
shelter, a place
to call home
as we cast our lines
toward
the distant horizon.

Acknowledgments

Marian Wright Edelman famously said it takes a village to raise a child. Well, it takes a crew to produce a book. I'd like to thank the talented student crew at Apprentice House – Kamryn Spezzano, Natalie Misyak, and Caitlyn Jennings – for their hard work and dedication, and director Kevin Atticks for captaining this project and giving my memoir a berth. I appreciate the support of the readers who generously contributed blurbs – Ellen Sherman, Fran Bartkowski, Lisa Sturm, and Rabbi Danny Moss. I'm grateful to my ACAP family, the Academy of Clinical and Applied Psychoanalysis, for teaching me how to listen. Special thanks to my husband, Bob Gerber, for his love and enthusiasm for and encouragement of my writing.

About the Author

Nancy Gerber is the author of five books of fiction and memoir, a book of poetry and short prose, and a scholarly monograph. She completed a Ph.D. in English at Rutgers University and a Certificate in Psychoanalysis at the Academy of Clinical and Applied Psychoanalysis, where she is a member of the faculty. She maintains a private therapy practice.

Apprentice
House Press
Loyola University Maryland

Apprentice House Press is the country's only campus-based, student-staffed book publishing company. Directed by professors and industry professionals, it is a nonprofit activity of the Communication Department at Loyola University Maryland.

Using state-of-the-art technology and an experiential learning model of education, Apprentice House publishes books in untraditional ways. This dual responsibility as publishers and educators creates an unprecedented collaborative environment among faculty and students, while teaching tomorrow's editors, designers, and marketers.

Eclectic and provocative, Apprentice House titles intend to entertain as well as spark dialogue on a variety of topics. Financial contributions to sustain the press's work are welcomed. Contributions are tax deductible to the fullest extent allowed by the IRS.

To learn more about Apprentice House books or to obtain submission guidelines, please visit www.apprenticehouse.com.

Apprentice House Press
Communication Department
Loyola University Maryland
4501 N. Charles Street
Baltimore, MD 21210
Ph: 410-617-5265
info@apprenticehouse.com•www.apprenticehouse.com

CPSIA information can be obtained
at www.ICGtesting.com
Printed in the USA
JSHW051216101222
34538JS00004B/269

9 781627 204781